# You Are Allowed, Life Is A Gift

## Also by Torry Fountinhead

The 7 Pillars Your Authentic Self Stands On
Part I of The Essential Companion Series

The Beauty, Part I of The Contemplation Series

The Soul's Openner – Enchanting The Soul to 'Being'

Part II of The Contemplation Series

Reach The Fountain of Youth

Part III of The Contemplation Series

Shush! It's a Secret, The Lake Hides His Dummy
Part of The Rainbow of Life's Secrets

Life, The Amazing Story
Part of The Rainbow of Life's Secrets

Poem: Good Enough, Part of Forever Spoken, The International Library of Poetry

A Tip of an Iceberg Meditations, a series of short books among are:

Is Forgiving a Riddle?

Momentary Thoughts

The Life The Heart Sprouts

For As It Is The Mind That Makes The Body Rich

Unveil From All The Coats, Sing Your Heart

and many more at work…

# *You are Allowed, Life is a Gift*

Part IV of "Contemplations" Series

# Torry Fountinhead

Airé Libré Publishing & Computing Ltd.

*Print Book ISBNs:*
*ISBN 10: 0-9781499-6-3*
*ISBN 13: 978-0-9781499-6-3*

*© 2011 Torry Fountinhead*
*All Rights of this work are Reserved. No part or whole may be used, copied or reproduced, stored in retrieval systems, or transmitted, in any form or by any means whatsoever, including electronic media, mechanical, photocopying, recording, or otherwise.*

*For more information contact:*
*Airé Libré Publishing & Computing Ltd.*
*Suite 306 , 185-911 Yates St.*
*Victoria BC V8V 4Y9 Canada*
*Tel: 1-250-592-3099.*
*http://www.al.bc.ca*
*info@al.bc.ca*

*Book Web-Site URLs:*
*http://youareallowedlifeisagift.torryfountinhead.ca*

*Part of:*
*http://contemplations.al.bc.ca*

*Dedication*

Cheers to Life!
May my words enlighten you and make your burdens lift, your foot lighter, as you walk on *YOUR* Path of this wonderful Life.

With Love & Light,

## *Table of Contents*

| | |
|---|---|
| *You are Allowed, Life is a Gift* | *i* |
| *Also by Torry Fountinhead* | *ii* |
| *You are Allowed, Life is a Gift* | *iii* |
| *Print Book ISBNs:* | *iv* |
| *Dedication* | *v* |
| *Table of Contents* | *vii* |
| *You are Allowed, Life is a Gift* | *xiii* |
| *Poem* | *xv* |
| *The Statements* | *1* |
| *PART 1* | *3* |
| *You are alive therefore, breathe.* | *4* |
| *Your breath is your evidence that you are allowed to live.* | *6* |
| *You were born therefore, you are allowed to live.* | *8* |
| *Raise you head high, you are walking upright.* | *10* |
| *You have the power of choice.* | *12* |
| *You have Free Will, exercise it.* | *14* |
| *Earth is your cradle too.* | *16* |

*You are unique, so you are allowed your
uniqueness.* 18

*You are gifted thus, you are allowed to exercise
your gifts.* 20

*You are allowed to be exactly as you are.* 22

*You are allowed to have knowledge.* 24

*You are allowed to have awareness.* 26

*You are deserving of the best.* 28

*Goodness is your heritage.* 30

*Well-Being is your heritage.* 32

*Success is inborn in you.* 34

*Laughter is your Human Nature.* 36

*Speech is your Human trait.* 38

*You are allowed to speak.* 40

*You are allowed to your opinions, whether or not
other agree with them or not.* 42

*You are allowed to be accepted, despite your
opinions.* 44

*You are allowed to be respected, and not being
taken for granted.* 46

*You are a child of The Creator, you deserve
respect.* 48

*You are allowed to be kind, but not by sacrificing yourself.*     50

*You are allowed to have alliances, but not by being taken advantage of.*     52

*You are allowed to be kind.*     54

*You are allowed to be thanked for each of your kindnesses.*     56

*You have a great value, this is a fact proven by your existence.*     58

*You are allowed to be appreciated.*     60

*You are allowed to move to your own drumbeat.*     62

*You are allowed to have your own rhythm.*     64

*Your greatness will shine when you are moving to your own rhythm.*     66

*You are allowed to decide about your own life.*     68

*You are allowed to choose your own livelihood.*     70

*Your time is for you to spend.*     72

*You are allowed to take a break.*     74

*Your thoughts are your own; you are allowed to keep them to yourself.*     76

*Your privacy is your own; no one can demand to know it.*    78

*Your ideas are your proof for direct connection to All-That-Is.*    80

*Your ideas are your own.*    82

*You are allowed to have your own special connection to All-That-Is.*    84

*You are allowed to know your own Truth.*    86

*You are allowed to learn from your own experience.*    88

*You are allowed to your own tastes.*    90

*You are allowed to have your own likes and dislikes.*    92

*You are allowed to be provided for.*    94

*You deserve to have all your needs taken care of.*    96

*You are allowed to be in Abundance and have Abundance.*    98

*You are allowed to give, but not take it away from yourself.*    100

*Tender Love & Care are your birthrights.*    102

*Your feelings & emotions are part of your tools; you are allowed to have them.*    104

*You are allowed to choose your feelings &*

| | |
|---|---|
| *emotions.* | *106* |
| *You are allowed to alter any of your feelings & emotions.* | *108* |
| *You are allowed to make mistakes, only they aren't mistakes, but new reference points.* | *110* |
| *You are allowed to lift you eyes and meet with appreciation in other's eyes.* | *112* |
| *Epilogue* | *115* |
| *PART 2* | *117* |
| *Joy is your inheritance.* | *118* |
| *You are allowed to be joyful at all times.* | *120* |
| *You were created powerful, you are entitled to your power.* | *122* |
| *You were created healthy, you are entitled to good health.* | *124* |
| *Freedom is your birthright.* | *126* |
| *You are allowed to live your life, as you wish, without hurting another.* | *128* |
| *You are allowed to have abundance flow to you and through you.* | *130* |
| *Your giving is you bearing fruits of your creation.* | *132* |

*You are allowed to have life's necessities, so you*

| | |
|---|---|
| *can be truly nourished.* | *134* |
| *Love is the substance of survival.* | *136* |
| *Love Thy Self, you are allowed to be loved.* | *138* |
| *Touch is the gift of existence upon Earth; you are allowed to be touched gently.* | *140* |
| *You live in a changeable world, you are allowed to change.* | *142* |
| *You are allowed to grow and develop.* | *144* |
| *You are allowed to choose your own path of evolution.* | *146* |
| *You are allowed to evolve.* | *148* |
| *You are allowed to gather your courage.* | *150* |
| *You are allowed to be courageous and extraordinary.* | *152* |
| *Inspiration is Spirit within you, you are allowed to have it.* | *154* |
| *You are full of light and allowed to shine it.* | *156* |
| *You are a beautiful creation of The Creator, let your beauty shine.* | *158* |
| *You are allowed to be beautiful.* | *160* |
| *Your own "You are allowed" statements 162-179* | |
| *Farewell* | *180* |

# You Are Allowed, Life Is A Gift

A breath of life

           - Wakeup

A man was created

           - Humanity

## The Statements

"The Statements", here there are appearing as the chapter names, but in reality – they are statements of Truth that should be acknowledged, and understood.

Unfortunately, a too large number of people do not even know it while, others might even go so far as to dispute them and thus, create suffering for themselves, or others.

Our minds, and our whole being, are capable to discern the Truth if faced with a statement, or a question, because it is our nature to explore.

Many a times, people would rather not deal with such truths, but by doing thus, they are limiting themselves, and their lives. In addition, they then also limit other in their environment.

The first step is to wake up from any and all trances induced by your own, or society's limiting belief systems, and look at your life.

Exercise your innate gift of exploration, be courageous, and face it – you would only gain joy and freedom from it, even in the midst of changes.

Let us embark in our explorations.

You are Allowed
Life Is A Gift

# Part 1

## You are Allowed Life Is A Gift

You are alive therefore,

        breathe.

And the LORD God formed man [of] the dust of the ground, and breathed into his nostrils the breath of life; and man became a living soul.

{Genesis 2:7}

It is of a wonder that living people have to be reminded to breathe. Our breath is our connection to Life and Creation. Without it, we shall simply not *be*.

It is a fact, that in order for us to live and operate this wonder that is our body – we have to breathe, and breathe well. Even a shallow breathing may adversely affect our health, and ability to think and perform.

Yet, the current hurried life style, the stress that exist in life's every aspect, the world's problems and threats – like a huge mountain to be climbed every day before one may attend to their personal life and needs. Good breathing begets relaxation, which begets rejuvenations, growth, and energy – all of which are necessary for living.

What more of a reason do you need then to slow down, breathe, feel that you are alive, rejuvenate your vitality, and know that you are walking and living.

 *You are Allowed*
*Life Is A Gift*

Your breath is your
evidence that you
are allowed to live.

So many people succumb to the feelings of 'not good enough', 'not deserving', 'sinful from birth' etc. etc. etc. Those feelings are based on belief systems instilled in them from the moments of conception, birth and with cultural prejudices, forgetting that the mere fact that they breathe – proves that they are alive – they do exist! This proves that they are allowed to live, as otherwise, they would not have been conceived to start with, or even survived the pregnancy, and birth.

Our existence, as living beings, is not depended on the vehicles – our parents – that have been utilized by Life to bring us forth.

For our existence, the life within us is evidence enough to attest as a sanction to live, breathe and be happy.

Ask any person to explain the miracle of the first or the last breathe. You may also ask our scientists to emulate it, but they too, will not be able to do so, if, and when, our time has come – to be born, or die.

Maybe we should consider the magical occurrence of our existence, as a permission *to be,* exactly because we were born, and our breathe – a continual reminder of it.

Take a deep breath – and live well.

*You are Allowed*
*Life Is A Gift*

You were born therefore, you are allowed to live.

In continuation to the reference of the miracle of conception, birth, and death, Human Beings may try to emulate our nature, but to no avail. Yes, I know that some people cloned sheep, and or other beings, but not Human Beings with souls.

Even looking at the story of Frankenstein, one may see how people tried to philosophically-handle a question of a human cloning. Would the creature have a soul, understanding, and empathy, capacity for joy, and ability to learn, reason, or carry responsibility?

Even the question of aborting a pregnancy, does not relate to the actual miracle of getting pregnant to start with. It is just denoting of the parent(s) preference to not having that that already had been created.

Even the inclination to find a purpose, or calling in life, setting goals, and having desires all denote that Life within the Human Being is pulsating upward, and onward.

We know that we exist; we know that we may strive.

We know that we are allowed to live, even if it is against the wishes of other people.

*You are Allowed  
Life Is A Gift*

Raise you head high, you are walking upright.

IV

You must admit, we, Human Beings, are different – not better, but different from all other creatures that are on this Earth.

Meerkats, bears, and some monkeys may be able to straighten up for a while, and walk on their hind legs, but Human Beings natural state of operation is walking on our two legs – the top limps are arms, and not forelegs.

This we do for so many eons of time, that we now benefit greatly from the vast span of our vision, our developed brain, and our ability to run as two-legged. Although we require rest in a reclined fashion, to give our spine time to loosen up, and relax, we feel that we are made to walk upright; we certainly do not feel comfortable crawling on our bellies.

In actuality, movement is our natural mode of operation. Our health, and systems like the Lymph system in our body, requires us to move, so they may work properly. Disease and discomfort are usually the result, and or exasperated with a sedentary lifestyle.

Standing tall, with head held up, wide back, and elasticity in our gait will ensure that the multitude of parts within our body are given the subtle movement they need, and the circulation of fluids of our body will flow freely.

*You are Allowed*
*Life Is A Gift*

You have
the power
of choice.

v

We, Human Beings are extremely powerful. We have the power of choice.

In every moment of our waking life, we make multitude decisions, just by the mere fact that we exercise our power of choice – may it be consciously, or unconsciously.

Anything we put our attention on, anything we invest, or spend, our thoughts on – affects destinies, and futures of the whole.

We can change our direction in life in a second, just by taking another direction – this is the result of the power of choice.

If we make a mistake, we can readjust. If we lost an opportunity, we can work at it some more. If we lost, we can gain by trying again.

The power of choice – or Free Will, allows us the freedom to participate, succumb, surrender, or fight.

We may also choose to be kind, generous, compassionate, and loving.

The power of choice helps us see Life as manageable, as pliable, and helps us therefore, to be part of a dance, in which we may also choose to be graceful.

*You are Allowed  
Life Is A Gift*

You have
 Free Will,
exercise it.

VI

Oxford dictionary's 1st definition of 'Will' is – "The faculty by which a person decides or is regarded as deciding on and initiating action *(the mind consists of the understanding and the will)*". It is true that one might engage in the many more aspects of the will, but for the sake of us understanding the most important point, let us refer just to this explanation.

We are born with a will that enables us to live, and act as needed, in our lives. This innate structure is also born free – without any pre-given compulsion to obey, or follow other's wishes. Our survival is our inner highest-most drive.

Therefore, we are born free to decide and act, to choose and carry that which we strive for.

We are born with our vehicle – our body, and a myriad of tools, in the form of gifts, talents, abilities, and discerning power to proceed with the necessary action to attain the best life we can. In actuality, it is a must for us to exercise our will, even if we will surrender it entirely to someone else's will. Exercising our free will is the mandate given to us at birth.

It is our responsibility to widen our knowledge, understanding, and abilities in order to do so best. Therefore, we must exercise our free will, so we may choose well!

 *You are Allowed  
Life Is A Gift*

Earth is your cradle too.

 VII

Our beautiful blue planet is a home to countless forms of life, and existences, of which we are but one. Although, we are just one form, we have equal right – equal, not more, or less. We also have equal right to all other members of Humanity.

We are though equipped with a mind that allows us to affect all other living forms on our planet, and here is the most important message – we cannot assume that we may take over, and rob the lives of others, and of Earth itself. Doing so will boomerang back to us all our wrongdoings.

We are given the gift of life here on Earth and thus, Earth cradles us lovingly, giving us all that she can. We may enjoy this immense gift of life, as well as Earth abundance, but remember that we are not alone.

We seem to feel that we are thrown into the wilderness of Life, without any means of survival, but we must free ourselves from this line of thought, acknowledging the inexhaustible abundance of Earth, as well as our major tool for survival – our minds.

We are equipped; in the same manner that Earth is equipped of regeneration, and rejuvenation. We are not useless and unimportant – we are equally important as all of life on Earth.

 *You are Allowed  
Life Is A Gift*

You are unique, so you are allowed your uniqueness.

 VIII

Further to the point made earlier, although, we are equal, and one singular form of existence, we are unique and precious.

Imagine yourself as a prism of a unique shape, in the same way that there are no two polished diamonds that are the same although, they might be similar. The prism, that you are, shines the light of Creation in your own peculiar way – the way that only you may shine – and this is why you are precious.

There are those who believe that we are insignificant, but I have observed, time and time again, how each one of us is necessary for Life to accomplish its scheme in the richest way possible. When we completed our part, we pass on.

Take upon yourself the responsibility of your importance to Life, and thus, acknowledge your importance to yourself – not in an arrogant manner, but in humbleness, and understanding that the song and dance of Life is made possible, and richer by your existence.

Find that which is truly agreeable to you, that which expands your horizons and being, the collection of parameters that will help you live life in the healthiest and happiest way – while harming no-one else. You exist thus, you meant to be here. You exist thus, you meant to contribute to Life.

 *You are Allowed*
*Life Is A Gift*

You are gifted thus,
you are allowed to
exercise your gifts.

 IX

Being unique also suggests that you are pre-equipped with the gifts, talents, and abilities required for you to bring forth your part to Life. Alas, these are in a potential form, and in need to be exercised to become powerful. Learning is the game of Life, as it leads us both to discover our abilities, as much as to bring them forth. How would you know that you have the ability to swim if you are not entering some body of water?

For many years, people sent their kids to study, trying to equip them with a sufficient amount of knowledge before they set out to live on their own. Yet it is the living of Life, the choices we make that direct us in certain direction, which allow for different opportunities to show themselves to us.

The aptitudes we have are not necessarily denoting on the gifts and talents that we have. For example, quick mathematical wits does not have to indicate a good basis for an accounted, it could show what is needed to be an innovative composer, in the same way that eye-finger quick coordination does not mean that you have to be a typist, but that you could easily become a pianist.

Finding that which is in the innermost of your being, and agreeable to your life, will tell the path you are to follow.

*You are Allowed*
*Life Is A Gift*

You are allowed
to be exactly
as you are.

 x

Since we are all unique, so would be our opinions, tendencies, and tastes.

There is nothing wrong in becoming a typist, if this is what brings you joy, and you can lead a happy life, with a minimum amount of stress. Only, if this is not the life that is agreeable to you, find another way to demonstrate this gift of quick eye-finger coordination – anything from playing a musical instrument, to writing your own novels, creating beautiful pottery, or even playing basketball.

The idea is to really find what you are, and the best way to exercise your abilities to be in line with it.

Here it is also important to acknowledge that you are the only one that may attest to what you are; Therefore, no one may dictate to you what you *should* be. Allowing others to dictate to you may bring you to a life that is actually a slow death, loaded with sufferings, both acknowledged and unacknowledged. Remember, the disease come from dis-ease.

Trying to be like others is, in itself, a slow death, because it stops you from searching within, as well as creating a fake you. Be yourself – you would be both loved and hated to the same degree, as being a fake.

*You are Allowed*
*Life Is A Gift*

# You are allowed to have knowledge.

XI

What is knowledge in actuality? It is information about specific subjects, known to men currently, of which you study to memorise, and understand it, to the best of your ability.

Alas, knowledge is really just the first step. This information requires you to be able to assimilate it, and therefore, use it, in the process of living thus, knowledge gets a degree of 'knowing', because it was applied. You may recite knowledge, but you speak from knowing. The next step, of course, will be learning from it, experiencing it, in life, which will purify it to the degree of wisdom.

Back to the first step of acquiring the knowledge, firstly, you are allowed to acquire knowledge, even if it is a threat to 'the old way', or to your elders, or superiors. The fact that we are given, from birth, a thinking mind, and a fruitful imagination coupled with curiosity, proves that we are meant to use it, and benefit our growth from it.

If everything is to be accomplished by one generation, and no one else is allowed to know more, Humanity's lifespan will consist of the total sum of two generations. Or maybe three – if some will rebel. Your indication that you have met a dictator, or an oppressor, is when they tell you to stop asking question, or stop learning, and then blame you for knowing nothing.

Find your way to learning – you are meant to widen your horizons, and grow to fulfill your potential.

 *You are Allowed*
*Life Is A Gift*

# You are allowed to have awareness.

 XII

Have you heard the figure of speech 'wake up and smell the coffee?' Well, not only the smell of coffee is refreshing, but also being present, and acknowledging the messages, which your senses deliver to you, is paramount to living well.

In being aware, I mean to refer to being conscious, not only physically, but also mentally, so you may live, refraining from becoming an automaton look-a-like.

Usually, the mundane daily life may induce a state of automatic responses, as well as expectations, and actions. In order to live well, it is required of us to use our mind, and to have the necessary awareness that will allow us to make the right choices for our highest good.

Demands of other people might stress us to the degree that we will start rushing in life to such an extent, which will cause us to resolve ourselves to be in a 'default' mode. A default mode means that you will, most probably, have a greater chance to repeat past mistakes, and certainly stop growing.

One must acknowledge the difference, and distinguish between a default mode to a 'second-nature', as second-nature behaviour denotes on a high level of expertise that allows one to be more graceful in their performance.

Awareness also allows you to exhibit your knowledge, apply it, and gain the best benefits from it.

 *You are Allowed  
Life Is A Gift*

# You are deserving of the best.

XIII

Look at all the abundance and riches of nature, all around you. Imagine that the teachings of old are true, the ones that state that God, The Creator, created all of this goodness, because he wanted to endow his love and thus, created the Human-Beings who had the capacity to appreciate it all.

The more you look around with appreciative eyes and mind, the more you will be able to see the goodness that surrounds you.

Surely, appreciation should be the correct response versus desolation. Surely, if you feel that you lack abundance, it can be simple to see that it is not because there is not enough, but maybe we have to learn better how to receive it.

From our creation we *are* deserving of the best otherwise, none of this abundance would exist. Our ancestors, the hunters and gatherers collected the food they ate, long before agriculture and industry – they had enough.

Of course, 'enough' is per expectations. Yet, what if enough would start with the thought that *Life is a Gift*, therefore, we are endowed with Goodness already, and we can already rejoice. Thereafter, we may extend ourselves, in numerous ways, as methods of receiving more to our personal lives.

 *You are Allowed  
Life Is A Gift*

Goodness is your heritage.

XIV

Continuing with the same line of thought, one has to acknowledge that we are born to an existence where all this abundance exists already. If it was not our heritage, it will all disappear prior to our births, or we would not be born to it.

The nature of heritage is the passing of from one generation to the next, both physical and spiritual endowments.

Repel the doubt that might be in your heart, or mind. Repel the notion that you are born to nothing and that if you will not create it – it would not be. The facts are speaking for themselves – Earth, and all that is on it, and in it, exists – it is inherently ours.

This is the main reason why we should take care not to ruin it for the generations to come, exactly because we received it freely, for our enjoyment – and not our greed.

We are passing through a most wonderful heritage, we may enjoy it while we here, and leave it pristine for future generations.

Regarding the Spiritual Heritage, it is because the physical heritage already exists that we are able to have a greater freedom of thought, to enhance our Spiritual growth – become wiser, kinder, and prolific, towards one and all.

 *You are Allowed
Life Is A Gift*

# Well-Being is your heritage.

XV

Part and parcel of the heritage we are born to is the right to a state of well-being.

If you observe the medical knowledge that is already understood, you will find that it is natural for our bodies, as well as nature to strive for rejuvenation, self-correcting, and growth. You may then conclude that disease is really dis-ease, and is unnatural.

If all is set with processes and procedures to support our rejuvenation, and natural healing, we have to accept that our natural innate state is of well-being.

Alas, Human Beings think that they know best, and arm themselves with incomparable methods of self-destruction, and self-sabotage, stemming from total arrogance, and disrespect both towards themselves, and Creation.

Somehow, it is easier for us Humans to resort to beliefs of 'suffering' and 'victim', or 'it will not happen to me', rather than look at what we do – and correct our own ways.

I am not saying that there are no situation where we have suffered in the hand of others – and many times with permanent damage, but one should ask why Human live as they live?

*You are Allowed  
Life Is A Gift*

Success is inborn
in you.

XVI

One other thing, which is innately born in us, is success. Of course, the measure of success is as per a Human's opinion, but ultimate success is not. With ultimate success, we can see that when babies are born typically, they proceed through given stages of development, right from the first smile to standing, crawling, and walking. We can observe the development of their mind, understanding, individualisation, and speech.

The innate need for growth and development, leads us to strive forward, sometimes upwards, and sometimes downward. Alas, any movement, whether conceived as failure or success, is just another reference point, from which we should learn to exercise our choices in a better way.

Society does try to impose on us its opinions and beliefs, regarding what is success, but in actuality, Life is the measure whether we are successful, or not. Trust that your innate given talents are leading you towards success, as much as you should distrust your habits, as they are, most of the time, leading you toward failure.

One should not only entertain the thought that success is the only thing that is worthwhile. Failure is as good a teacher – if we listen, and learn. You may say therefore, that success is an understanding of each step of your journey, and adjusting your direction is the ultimate successful step you can take, on your way to your Highest Good, regardless of what is involved in the adjusting – pain, sorrow, or any other challenge.

*You are Allowed*
*Life Is A Gift*

# Laughter is your Human Nature.

XVII

It is quite fascinating that medicine discovered that when we smile, and even laugh, our system releases endorphins that make us feel better. Therefore, a smile – whether given with joy or fear, will still generate those endorphins, and brings us a sense of well-being.

Joy is our essence. Just look at a baby, and try to measure its development, you will see that the joyful baby has a lead on any subdued baby.

Laughter is the product of the bubbling joy within us, and when expressed, it will also bring joy to others around us. Laughter is meant to be shared. Either with other people or just with the environment that surrounds you.

When we speak of Human Nature, we do give a serious thought to that which is part of our makeup – which no operation can remove. Alas, we know of situations of torture, and abuse, that – for a time only – are capable of 'controlling' a person expression, but remove those shackles, and voilà, Human Nature is expressed freely again.

Norms of society do suppress the natural expression of laughter, instead of using it as a measure, and an indicator of how does a given situation affects the person involved. Just remember, that laughter may be induced by more than just joy, fear and ridicule might do it too.

*You are Allowed*
*Life Is A Gift*

Speech is your
Human trait.

XVIII

All in Creation communicates, whether we would like to acknowledge it, or not. The methods of communication differ, as per the need, survival mechanism, and aspirations of the organism.

We, the Human Beings, eons ago, decided that for our own benefit, and wishes, we will develop our speech ability, more than is required for our survival in nature.

We found that we have an extensive ability to form many types of movements with our tongue, in addition to producing sounds with our vocal cords – even if we did not know the mechanics of it. We found that we could find an outlet, and expression, for our thoughts.

Thus, speech was born.

Speech, like all of our modes of expression, was now affected by our choices, understanding, and personal nature. We could be kind or harsh, tolerant or impassionate, soft or loud, and so on, it could denote maturity, or juvenility.

You can gather that speech is a mode of expression and thus, all the responsibility for its usage lies with the person, and not with anyone else, including when one is in a reactionary mode.

Therefore, take care with this trait.

 *You are Allowed  
Life Is A Gift*

# You are allowed to speak.

  XIX

Following the definition of speech as a trait, one should now understand that it is a tool for us to use for our self-expression. Therefore, while adhering to certain decorum, we are allowed to demonstrate our uniqueness in saying both our opinions, aspirations, and sharing of our feelings.

The old habit of parents, demonstrated in the saying that children are to be seen, and not heard, definitely has stumped many creative thoughts, and inspirations, as well as created an emotional distance between the persons involved.

We are creative beings; we are also born to share just by the mere fact that we are part of society – large or small. The progress demonstrated by Humanity for millennia, required sharing of thoughts, ideas, practices, resources, and much more, in order to come forth.

It is quite fascinating to observe how parents might be impatient with their kids while, they can stand listening, and watching TV, radio, or movies for hours on hand. Where did the intuitive understanding of what is important gone?

Remember the saying 'From the mouth of babes...' well, although, children lack in experience, they are far more equipped than we allow it, to understand. Therefore, take the trouble of explaining – it is like seeding their minds.

*You are Allowed*
*Life Is A Gift*

You are allowed to your opinions, whether or not other agree with them or not.

xx

Your experience in life is your own; there is no equivalent to it, because of your uniqueness, and individuality. Although, two people may go through a similar experience, at the same time, the effect of it will differ for each one of them.

Imagine us not as identical holograms of the Whole, but as different prisms reflecting Life – each prism with its own shape, or size. Therefore, as much as ten separate artists, sitting in front of the same sunset, will paint it differently, so would your experience will be painted inwardly.

If you remember this about yourself – please also remember it regarding others. Each one of us is a conglomeration of the sum of our experiences, melding with our personality, individuality, constitution, and many things that are more particular.

If we understand the importance for sharing, and progress, we will allow for the differences with alacrity. We will enthusiastically welcome the variations, as they, in themselves, will induce creativity in us.

Think of other people's opinions, as the richness of nature, with its multitude shades of each colour. No one green shade ever hurt another, nor would another opinion will hurt you , unless, you will take it personally.

 *You are Allowed*  
*Life Is A Gift*

You are allowed
to be accepted,
despite your
opinions.

 XXI

Your being is entirely different from the opinion you hold – whether you express them, or not. Your being has irrevocable value regardless of your experiences, and whatever you go through, at any given moment.

Therefore, you should be accepted based on your value, as a Human Being, and not because of what opinions you hold, or what tastes you have.

Can you imagine a mother refusing to breast-feed her offspring just because it might have smiled at another? Can you imagine army conscription applying only to people of certain opinions? Can you imagine voting rights granted only to people who hold only the right kind of opinions?

I can hear your chuckle, so why would you doubt your right to be accepted, whether you do, or do not, express your opinions?

The importance, to adhere to here, is to accept people, and know that the differences that exist, treated gently, can only help all to grow, while learning to become gentler, calmer, and more reflective than reactive.

There is no need to try to convince anybody that *your* opinion is the Right One. You are the only one that may decide for yourself whether to keep *your* opinion, or change it, as per *your* experience.

*You are Allowed  
Life Is A Gift*

You are allowed to be respected, and not being taken for granted.

 XXII

Ask: what is a person – if not a recognised entity?

Ask: can one ask to be respected, if the same one does not respect another, or by what right one may feel valued, if the same one takes another for granted?

Following all that I have said up until now, you may conclude that I highly value any single Human Being, regardless of their creed, gender, colour, or what have you.

We may progress in Life, on our own path, and with our own aspirations, only when we start from an equal footing, because otherwise we are just fooling ourselves thinking that we have achieved it all. Think of a ladder, by climbing up another rung you accomplish something, while pushing the person in a higher rung lower – you still remain on the same level – no change thus, no accomplishment.

Imagine how much further in Life we will all advance, and with what ease if we assume that each person lives for a reason, whether we know what the reason is, or not. Each person has a value, which is to be contributed to Life, and thus, enhance life for all. No person has the right, or even the cognitive ability, to judge another's life importance, or value.

 *You are Allowed
Life Is A Gift*

You are a child of
The Creator, you
deserve respect.

XXIII

Each one of us was created for a reason, and this is reason enough to be respected, if we know what the reason is, or not.

Let me illustrate a weird analogy, if the meat eating Human Beings acknowledge and value, each animal that is available for their consumption, without comparison that is not within specific parameters. For example, they do not compare Lamb knuckles stew to a beefsteak, nor do they even compare Veal Parmesan to a regular beefsteak, so why would they question a person's value where there are even no specific parameters to aid us, only very general ones.

Most other people we see, or experience, it is usually only for a moment, and even those close to us are still somewhat remote to us. Therefore, we do not have the greater viewpoint to discern what is actually the other person's value, or reason for existence. For that matter – can we even say for sure, what our own reason for existence is?

Imagine a life, while walking on your journey's path, where you will try to discover your own value and reason for existence, without being engaged in other people Lives' reason. You will be capable to flow in Unison with the others, similarly to a flock of Starlings in flight, or a shawl of fish at sea. In reality, you will have a lot of time and energy to evolve – not wasting it on trivia.

*You are Allowed*
*Life Is A Gift*

You are allowed to be kind, but not by sacrificing yourself.

XXIV

There are two types, at least, of being kind. The one is expressing yourself in a kind manner, whether toward yourself, another, or the world. The second type is by rendering kindness where it is needed.

When you are unkind in your expression, you are bordering on abuse, because you cannot have dominion over others – the Creator is the only one who has this prerogative. Unkindness in speech will always translate to criticism, as much as unkindness in behaviour will be translated to selfishness, and arrogance.

Rendering kindness should only be done while taking a full account of your own resources and abilities, physical, mental, and emotional. Self-sacrificing will always happen if you render more than you have, and the first sufferer will be *you*.

We are not born to be serfs, or minions, or slaves, or whatever name you want to call the bondage people put on others, in order to gain what they themselves do not have, or do.

That Humanity has such a history only denotes on the poor humane feelings of it. Just imagine a lord becoming a serf – how would he feel?

Give; be kind, only do it safely, and reasonably.

 *You are Allowed
Life Is A Gift*

You are allowed to have alliances, but not by being taken advantage of.

 XXV

The value of a Human Being cannot be disputable. Even when one person takes advantage of another, by their actual act it proves the value of the other person.

This is where it is so important to acknowledge that the person being taken advantage of might carry some self-diminishing beliefs, and or mistaken their own value.

The old adage 'it takes two to Tango' applies here; one person think in superiority manner, and the other thinks in inferiority one. The myriad of societies on Earth show us that, everywhere we know, people fight each other, they also create false class systems and thus, it seems one should fall into one definition, or another, willingly or not.

Alliances are born when people acknowledge the value of the other, and therefore, form an alliance, so both sides may enjoy and profit by it.

Like a stress being applied on an iron rod will eventually break the rod, so a person being taken advantage of will eventually fall ill, or rebel, or both. Either way, the alliance will cease to exist, and so will the benefits that could have been derived from it.

Alliances' base is value and trust.

*You are Allowed*
*Life Is A Gift*

You are allowed to be kind.

XXVI

You are allowed to be kind; it is a sign of a generous heart, and not of weakness.

Is it not funny how people will accept harshness so easily, but will suspect kindness?

Why does Harshness seem to be a sign of superiority, and kindness of inferiority?

To be kind, as discussed earlier, denotes self-confidence – the knowing that you have a full heart, and willing to share from its fullness.

Look at nature, where animals are not threatened, they walk peacefully, and share the environment. Surely, Human Beings should gravitate towards kinder environment, to save themselves from being stressed continuously.

Many a times, it is in competitive environments that people tend to criticise, blame, and become harsh. They think that it will be the only way to survive alas it is the opposite. Kindness will promote the sense of security and trust, and therefore, will be a good breeding ground for collaboration, and or even working by oneself more productively.

Kindness allows people to concentrate better on their own life's work, and therefore, enhances the chance for greater fulfillment of the individual.

 *You are Allowed*
*Life Is A Gift*

You are allowed
to be thanked
for each of your
kindnesses.

 XXVII

What is it actually to give thanks?

When a person is capable of feeling that they were benefited, they will naturally feel gratitude. When the feeling of being benefited is being delayed, due to any one of a myriad of reasons, gratitude is slow to come – if it comes at all.

If we will keep in mind that we do not always know why, or how, things transpire in Life, we will welcome any kindness with thanks regardless, if we already feel the benefit, or not.

Imagine a scenario where you can already see yourself thanking another, or thanking Life, for having that which you heart desires, or the need has been fulfilled, and joy is running in your veins. It does beg the question what comes first, the thanking for the fulfillment, or the manifestation of it.

Like the chicken and the egg, who comes first is open for discussion, but because we operate on many levels, of which the physical is but one, could it be that giving the thanks first will only seem that way. Inwardly, we might already have asked unknowingly, and giving thanks may be thanking whatever the outcome will be.

Thanking for kindness welcomes any outcome.

 *You are Allowed*
*Life Is A Gift*

You have a great
value, this is
a fact proven
by your existence.

 XXVIII

There is nothing in Creation that has no part to play – all is designed and calculated to the minute details.  If it is the birds that eat the Locusts and thus, protect the crops that Human Beings depend on for their staple diet, or even be the Dragon Fly that is not only beautiful, but feeds on the Mosquitoes that otherwise, will sting us to great sufferings.

The value assigned to each part of Creation is beyond our understanding, as we are not aware of the greater picture that paints all the dependencies between each part.  The fact that we might not understand it, does not give us the right to dismiss it, as unimportant.

We live in a world of duality, which means that in our reality all has a point of reference.  We would not know that something is long, if there was not a short to show its relation to it, nor would we will be able to value the good, if there was not bad to highlight it for us.

Therefore, while you exist, you can be sure (and so everybody else that knows or meets you) that you have a part to play and thus, you have a value – you mere existence is the proof of it.

Yes, I know of the atrocities committed, past and present, trying to show that some people had better not exist, but that could only be done because they have been assigned a value, if they were valueless, no one would bather about them.

 *You are Allowed  
Life Is A Gift*

You are allowed to be appreciated.

 XXIX

Continuing with the understanding that you are valuable, should you not also see that you have the innate right to be appreciated. That is not to say that you are allowed to demand it – but if you find yourself unvalued, choose to leave the place, or situation.

It reminds me of a story I have heard of a teacher that used the analogy of the hidden treasure. In the days when we still rode in horse and carriage, the streets were full of horse droppings, and the teacher said, imagine that in each dropping there is hidden a nugget of gold – imagine each person you see, as if he is a nugget of gold. By the way, all the mushrooms we eat and think of as delicatessen are grown on horse manure.

It is of utmost importance that you will appreciate yourself first, because where ever you go, and to whom ever you speak, you convey this inner acknowledgement of your own value and thus, they may respond to it – favourably and appreciatively, or not, but if you present yourself as lowly, they might be tempted to agree with you.

Accept votes of appreciation, as long there are truthful and sincere. Remember that you have inwardly something that can benefit the world, treat yourself, and others gently.

Be graceful in your acceptance.

*You are Allowed*
*Life Is A Gift*

You are allowed to move to your own drumbeat.

xxx

Although, we are all equal, we are not exactly the same, as discussed previously – we are all unique. Sometimes, people will say that they are wired differently, but in reality, they just denote the difference.

What is different about us is the frequency in which we vibrate. This frequency creates the unique field we operate in, and put into musical terms, exhibits itself like a drumbeat.

Each particular frequency will gravitate toward complementary frequencies, and when it is not complementary – this is where people would say 'Oh, he is following his own drumbeat'.

Your frequency is uniquely yours, given to you at the moment of your creation. Do not feel guilty, or ashamed of it, you are allowed to be you. You are allowed to your own uniqueness, regardless if it agreeable to others, or not.

We are all of different physical, emotional, and mindful constitutions, and designed for different purposes. There is not such a thing as 'normal'; you cannot conform to that which you are not.

Go against your grain, and you will jeopardise your health, and life. Follow your own drumbeat, and be healthy, and productive.

*You are Allowed  
Life Is A Gift*

# You are allowed to have your own rhythm.

XXXI

Your rhythm stems from your frequency, and constitutional particulars. For example, in athletics, you may easily differentiate between a long distance runner and a sprinter. These days, the medical professionals even know that the muscle structure of these athletes is fundamentally different, so you cannot even turn one type to be the other.

How many times have you heard people say that they either a 'morning person', or 'a night owl'. It all goes back to our uniqueness represented in our constitution.

When conforming to mass beliefs, and work places, this element of trying to equalise conditions is what causes the fractures in one's health – and left for long – breaks the person.

On the other hand, if one lives and works with the best conditions to their own highest good, the value of this person will then shine, and bestowed on everyone. What a marvellous gift would it be?

It is your responsibility to 'know thy self' therefore, take the time to learn yourself. Understand that you can only bring forth the best in you, if you adhere to your own rhythm. You can only be happy, evolve, and progress in life if you listen within, and follow your own rhythm – let your drum beat to its true marching sound.

 *You are Allowed  
Life Is A Gift*

Your greatness will shine when you are moving to your own rhythm.

 XXXII

Let us say that you have discovered your own rhythm, because you took the time to listen within, and have registered in your mind what was agreeable to you, and what was not.

Let us also make sure that we take out of the equation the fear argument, as sometimes you might feel at odds, because you just fear the outcome, or the unknown.

Imagine that you are the *master* of your own *being*. Imagine that the Life Force streaming in your veins freely and you are ready to follow your inspiration, with right action.

The power you feel within is the power resulting from being true to yourself. Unlike the short-term power, you feel when you apply force, to yourself, or another.

This is the strength of your resolve, and self-assurance. Being steadfast is being assured at the way you would go about achieving your aspiration, and keeping at it.

Your greatness stems from all of this. You can only be great when you are true to yourself, have the power and inspiration, and look ahead to your aspiration. Joy will be the added result to your mission fulfilled. Yet, although success is never a promise, in a way, you are successful when you acted truthfully.

*You are Allowed*
*Life Is A Gift*

# You are allowed to decide about your own life.

 XXXIII

You are born, going through the birth canal by yourself – even twins are born one at the time. You also die by yourself, even if you are not the only person dying at the time.

You are the only one who can live your life; no one else can, or may, live it for you. Even the food and water that you consume can only be consumed by yourself – even the baby's breast milk.

I guess you get the point I am trying to convey, that you are the only one who can live your life, so is it not also quite clear that all the choices you make, or allow (give the sanction to) someone else to make on your behalf – are your responsibility.

You certainly 'suffer' the consequences of those miscalculated choices, and enjoy the good results of the educated ones.

See your life, as your own to live. See your life, as your own to make decisions about, even if they do not agree with other people's opinions.

You are like a tool – if used well, the work is done well, if used badly undesired results may ensue.

Make it your mission to know thyself to such an extent that you would be able to 'drive' yourself in the best way possible.

 *You are Allowed*
*Life Is A Gift*

You are allowed to choose your own livelihood.

 XXXIV

Ask yourself, what is livelihood? Hopefully, you will arrive at the conclusion that in order to survive, you must engage in some kind of activity, which will facilitate you getting your needs taking care of.

You will find that it is your individuality, abilities, gifts, talents, and joy that may lead you to a short list of activities, which might become the theme of your livelihood.

Here we should also acknowledge, in extremes, how working hard at a subject you love, will lead you to joy and evolution while, working hard at a subject you disdain, can come close to slavery, not to mention the reduction in emotional, psychological, and physical health. In addition, the rate of your contribution to yourself, family, and society at large, directly affected by your choice of livelihood.

We should also mention that sometimes, a person might have the aptitude to perform a certain type of job, but in actuality the aptitude is there, because the same talents are required for a different job altogether. This usually lead to errors of judgement, both on your own behalf, as well as the people who seem to know you.

Do not make the mistake of choosing by default – make a point to follow you heart to joy – and not to a heart-ache.

*You are Allowed*
*Life Is A Gift*

Your time is for you to spend.

XXXV

From conception to birth, you have to spend your time in tandem with you mother, but once born, you start to dictate your own time activities. No parent will stop the baby from falling asleep, nor would have the peace of mind to ignore the squalls of food demanding.

Yes, you have to oblige caregivers, school schedules, and the like, but in essence – you are there therefore, you made the choice to be there. How many people have we heard of that skip school, or instead of sleep, walk the streets? Of course, this kind of behaviour is questionable, but what I am trying to illustrate is that you are driven to do that which you deem right for you.

While growing, and becoming an adult, it is more obvious that you are in charge of your commitments, and choices – and this is a most important time to realise that your time is yours to spend. In the same way that no one else may live your life for you, no one is capable of spending your time for you.

If you are, you are spending your time. If you live, you live through spending your time in whatever activity.

Therefore, be cognisant of your priorities, tastes, and needs, and thus choose the activities you spend your time on – carefully.

 *You are Allowed  
Life Is A Gift*

# You are allowed to take a break.

XXXVI

Hear this clearly – 'not doing' is also 'doing'. Rest is also an activity. Please do not mistake physical activity to be the only type of activity there is. We are far more complex beings, and we have inner-goings and invisible activities all the time, even while we are performing physical activities.

Ask yourself, what is a break? You might naturally arrive at the spontaneous answer that you have felt like arriving at an end of something, and needed a break.

While we live, we are also maintaining our bodily processes, mind experiences, emotional loads, and much more. We are in constant communication with our inner-self, which leads us to acknowledge a need to take a break.

Remember, the highest priority of our 'being' is to be able to carry on 'being', and thus that which is necessary for it to keep our equilibrium, inner balance, good health etc. will dictate when brakes are needed. Alas, work places, spouses, children, and others put such demands on us that cause us, many a times, to ignore these internal communications.

The value in a rest is our ability to allow our creative part to come to the fore, and assimilate, digest, absorb, inspire, resolve, remember, and much more. This allow us to be inventive, more productive, and certainly on our way to a better success.

*You are Allowed  
Life Is A Gift*

Your thoughts are your own; you are allowed to keep them to yourself.

XXXVII

Regardless of whom do we think generate the thoughts that are passing through our minds, while they are there – they are ours to keep and observe – personal, private, and cherished.

Our mind has a background, like a blue clear sky, of which the thoughts are passing through it like the clouds. Some are fleeting, and some create a heavy over-cast.

Relate to your thoughts as indicators, on the one hand reflecting your emotional responses in thoughts format, and on the other hand engaged in efforts to understand, ponder, and find solutions and so on.

Our thoughts are, in actuality, in a non-finished format, so sharing them might bring in consequences, as per the company, or the subject.

Musing is a very personal activity to be cherished. Remember that once you pronounce your thoughts with words – you energise them, so positive ones are endowed with power, as well as the negative ones.

Many people speak out loud the content of their thought, or feelings, before considering if they are kind, and just to do so. If something, by nature, is private, question first if it should be shared, or exposed.

*You are Allowed  
Life Is A Gift*

Your privacy is your own; no one can demand to know it.

XXXVIII

People forget that we comprise many layers, multitude of reflections, and sublime understandings, to say the least. We are complex beings, living in the moment, but yet, living on many layers – of many moments.

How many times did you say something only to witness another's response that seemed to be out of place?

You, and I, and everybody else, cannot reveal ourselves entirely, at any one point in time. In addition to that, each person has his/her own way, and level, of understanding.

Trying to reveal ourselves may bring on additional challenges while, responding with a relevant context, may constitute a productive communication.

We may also be in the process of assimilating some things of our lives, and are not ready with explanations, reasons, or justifications.

The external dress code should also apply to the inner dress code, and even be much more modest. In the same way you are not expected to show off your 'private parts' in company, you also *should not* be expected to 'undress' your inward being.

The concept of privacy was created, so people would respect each other, and have healthy boundaries – stepping on toes is not to be part of the game of life – only a poor 'dancer' does that.

 *You are Allowed  
Life Is A Gift*

Your ideas are
your proof for
direct connection to
All-That-Is.

 XXXIX

Being held in the cradle of Creation, we have the ability to flow with 'Life', or resist it. While flow requires Trust and Resolve, resisting will just delay our growth, expansion, and joy.

When one's mind is in the grip of fear, or some obsession, it actually stops our flow, and ability to be communicated with.

Real flow is like a gentle scanning of all that surrounds us, as well as concerns us. It is done mostly in subtle ways, under the surface, and many a time in unknown ways. It is the dominion of our deep consciousness, so it may be able to help us go forth.

Ideas are like sparks of light that shines through the leaves of our streaming thoughts. These light-sparks come to us, because we are a fertile soil – a ready soil, to receive these seeds.

There is a constant communication, give and take, a dance like interaction between us and Creation, and all that is within it therefore, it is a requirement to be in a flow, in order to be in a receptive mode.

Like our breath, inhale and exhale, the exhale is a required letting go, before we may receive the breath once more.

Ideas, like breath, can only come in while in the flow, so dance with Life forever more.

*You are Allowed*
*Life Is A Gift*

Your ideas are
your own.

XL

You succeeded to receive those Light-Sparks, the ideas are showing up in your mind, so firstly enjoy and bask in the feeling of this streaming.

Recognising the streaming, and giving attention to it, will help it become second nature, which will allow you to reinstate it more freely in the future.

Being the 'fertile soil' that received these ideas determines your own readiness, and no one else's. Therefore, you are the one granted the gift, and as the gift is yours, these ideas are yours to act upon.

There is nothing wrong with sharing your ideas. Yet, reflect upon it, does anything come out of this sharing? If you achieved satisfaction by sharing, or you acted upon the ideas, all is well, but if by sharing you let your energies evaporate with them, it will be like leaving the seeds in the dry soil and never watering them, to help them sprout.

You may not be able to act on your ideas, and I would like to suggest that by conceiving them, you already benefited the world – idea conceived, is an idea born to the Universal Mind. You may actually witness someone else acting on it although, you conceived it. The idea is yours for a time, and then it is going forth to the world.

*You are Allowed*
*Life Is A Gift*

You are allowed
to have your own
special connection
to All-That-Is.

XLI

To describe your connection to All-That-Is in a succinct way is to say that each and every particle, including you, of Creation is an essential part of it. Creation cannot be the same without any, which is created within it.

Like a drop in the ocean that helps make the ocean, you are counted, cherished, and valued. Like the drop in the ocean, you are to flow with it, whether with the tides of calm waters, or in a storm.

No one, but no one, is allowed to, or has the sanction to doubt the importance of your existence, the rightness of your being, or to extinguish you, although, we do know of atrocities where people do just that, on their own accord.

Being part of creation, you have a particular and individual connection whether, you acknowledge it, or not. In the same way that you are the only one thinking your own thoughts, breathing your own breaths, and conceiving your own ideas – you are singularly connected.

All of the above grants you the sanction to be continuously connected, and benefited directly. It is though, up to you to maintain the openness of mind, and to be in receptive mode.

Never doubt your connection, as well as never close yourself up to it.

*You are Allowed  
Life Is A Gift*

You are allowed
to know your own
Truth.

XLII

Previously, I illustrated you as a prism, shining the Light in your own special way, which also means that you have a unique way of understanding, and discernment.

When I speak of your own truth, I refer to the way you discern the Truth, from your own point of view, belief systems, and moods.

No one can walk in your own shoes, per se, they can sympathise, have compassion, be angry with you, or criticise you, but they cannot duplicate you.

Your truth, far more than gravity, is what keeps you standing-up while in the present – it is this that grounds you. It is only when you are grounded that you can make sound decisions, best for that time.

Even if someone might challenge your stance, be assured that you have the right to be, and to be as you are, at that moment. Each moment of your being is the jumping board – the start point of the next moment. You are continuously growing, and changing. You, of yesterday, is not the you of today.

Remember to keep an open heart, open mind, and welcome change while, understanding your own truth.

 *You are Allowed*
*Life Is A Gift*

You are allowed
to learn from your
own experience.

XLIII

Let me say, today is Monday therefore, tomorrow will be Tuesday alas, only when tomorrow comes, and you actually experience it – it is Tuesday *indeed*.

Experience really means living through something, which leaves its impressions on you, in countless ways.

The impression the experience leaves on you, on your many levels, is the lesson not only of that day, but also of many days to come, because we do live by comparisons, and associations.

Continuing the understanding of your uniqueness, only you can learn from your experience. This is not to say that you cannot share your learning, later on, even teaching it to others, but for them it will only become 'indeed', if and when they will go through a similar experience.

This is when you will really need your own time, breaks, contemplation, and self-understanding, and should not compromise yourself in the process.

We are living; we are here, to evolve. We can only evolve if we pay attention, and learn from our experiences otherwise, the same experiences will repeat themselves again, and again, until we do.

*You are Allowed
Life Is A Gift*

You are allowed to your own tastes.

XLIV

How fascinating society is in its judgments and criticism, do you see it as a wonder?

Each person has their own taste buds in their mouth, and they have their own unique formations of rods and cones in their physical eyes, so how could anyone assume that even two people could have *identical* tastes?

The pros and cons that built society originally, promote uniformity versus variety.

Alas, the more society fights against uniqueness, and individual realisation, the more it facilitates resentment, fear, and general negativity.

Instead, realise that you are unique, and so is everybody and everything else in creation. Realise that each is a gift, and part of the puzzle that builds the image of your reality. Assume that adventure of discovery is a good experience, and choose joy as your companion, instead of dread.

When you taste something new, and do not like it, gently refrain from assaulting your taste buds, and gently excuse yourself from eating it, so as *not* to insult your provider. If you see something that disturbs you, ask within, why does it disturb you could it be that you judge, or fear it? Could it be that you forgot to be more accepting?

Remember, uniqueness is an adventure, enjoy it.

*You are Allowed*
*Life Is A Gift*

You are allowed to have your own likes and dislikes.

XLV

What are 'likes' and 'dislikes'? In reality, due to your own experiential existence, and your own taste buds and five senses particulars, you build, through time, an inner library of knowledge that records your likes and dislikes.

This same library was created for our protection, and personal growth, as it also houses the knowledge of 'not putting your hand in the fire', 'not jumping over a cliff without a parachute of sorts', and so on.

A very nice attribute of this library is the ability to re-write previous interpretations of your senses, as per new experiences, or some personal training.

There is nothing wrong in trying again to test something, there is, on the other hand, major wrong in forcing yourself, due to someone else's 'requirement'.

Just remember, that your own likes and dislikes are not written in stone, they are entirely open to change – by you alone.

Likes and dislikes also provide you with an obvious imagery of your own critical, and or judgemental nature. Remember that you are allowed to change your opinions – you are allowed to develop and grow.

*You are Allowed  
Life Is A Gift*

# You are allowed to be provided for.

XLVI

Think of your most primary physical activity – your breathing. Breathing is a requirement of Life; you cannot exist here on Earth, as a Human Being, otherwise.

Humans do not supply the air you breathe freely, although, it may be fouled by them. The air you breathe is *provided* freely in the environment of Earth.

What if all your other physical, emotional, and spiritual requirements are working on the sane basis as air?

What if there is an endless supply of energy that can transform to the particular requirement needed for your survival?

What if Human Beings gathered to form societies, so they would be able to contribute to each other in such a way that will provide for the survival requirements of each part of it? An example would be parents, and their children.

Imagine that each person has the ability, if not yet the full knowledge, of transforming the Universe's free energy in such a way that actually reveal to all their talents, gifts, aptitudes, and tendencies. With this information, people may get together, and benefit from each other's presence in their lives. We are both providers and provided.

 *You are Allowed  
Life Is A Gift*

You deserve to have all your needs taken care of.

XLVII

Continuing with the theme of provision, one can see the importance of each person, to the best of their ability, being both providers, and provided for.

Needless to say, that the exchange is not with an identical item, but with a 'valued' item.

In addition, those who are left by the sidelines, and their existence's needs are ignored, are not able to contribute productively to the society, and or the environment they live in.

One may ask, so why do they breathe, if it was not to give them life? Why do they still walk the Earth, if not to grace it with their gift?

I mentioned earlier in 'Success is inborn in you' that we are innately striving for growth therefore, each person should strive to learn how to transform the energy in such a way, as to bring forth their own gifts, as well as be helped in contributing them to Life.

Each person's gifts and contributions should be valued, and appreciated – this where criticism is damaging rather than promoting.

'Love thy neighbour as thy self' shows in this case, how important we are to each other. Mutual support is vital to Life.

*You are Allowed*
*Life Is A Gift*

You are allowed
to be in Abundance
and
have Abundance.

XLVIII

Relate abundance to flow, and remember the flow of air in an open environment.

It is you that needs to flow like the air in an open environment. It is you that when flowing, you will exhibit all that you are, and grace the world with your gifts.

When you are in the flow, you are able to be creative versus be in a state of stuck that leads to stagnation.

Previously I compared the abundance in your environment etc. to express how we should look at abundance as the basic occurrence in Life. Now, it is imperative for you to acknowledge that if you will remember to be **in** the flow – abundance, you may then also **receive** a flowing abundance.

Life is an experiential adventure, which exposes us to myriad of occurrences. The only way for us live life fruitfully is to respond in kind therefore, flow with it, express yourself creatively, gift and grace the world with your speciality.

Abundance may flow to you, and through you, as long as neither you, nor another, put a dam to block it – totally, or partially.

Look at your life, and distinguish how well in the flow you are.

 *You are Allowed  
Life Is A Gift*

You are allowed
to give, but not
take it away from
yourself.

 XLIX

Once, I spoke to a loved wise man about love and marriage, what does facilitate a sound partnership, and he took a moment before responding. He chuckled, and said that, as it so happens; people should learn Physics before embarking on any relationship.

His theory was simple. In nature, and therefore in Physics, there is no natural vacuum. Each person should bring an equal part to any relationship namely, 50% each, so to make 100% total for the relationship, for it to survive. Alas, in many partnerships, one person will bring less. At the same time, the other person's love and wish for the partnership to be sustained, will invest more than their expected 50%, and that amounts to taking more from the self.

The partnership/Marriage, when is based on the 100% whole, sustains the two people involved, nourishes them, and help them evolve. On the other hand, when one gives more than the other does, you have a relationship of a taker and giver. Invariably, this leads to depletion, causing ill health, and even divorce.

The Balance (scale), when balanced can maintain the storms of life, but when tilted – it will just fall down. Human Beings must maintain their own balance, so not to fall… Be aware of your own capacities, and keep centred.

 *You are Allowed Life Is A Gift*

Tender Love &
Care are your
birthrights.

 L

"Moderation is the key to inner Peace", did you know that?

It is not an accident that Human Beings are born as delicate babies, in need of tender love and care. Can you imagine a baby treated differently, and remain alive, healthy, or sane?

The baby's need of gentleness, in all respects, is to set us, the adult caregivers, in a mode of gentleness alas, somehow we change our behaviour towards adults.

We all have still the child in us, the one that can get hurt – so very easily, even if we put on masks, and bold responses. Every day we go through many experiences, which challenge our energy reserves while taxing our patience, choice making, and equilibrium.

We are far more vulnerable than we would like to admit, and if admitting, our fellow man will regard us as weaklings.

Yet, the facts speak for themselves namely, people who are treated in a gentle way, respond far better to those who are being bullied. Stress in life does not induce productivity, but suffering.

Demands put on a person, which exceed the abilities of that person to maintain his/her equilibrium, will cause them to break up.

*You are Allowed  
Life Is A Gift*

Your feelings & emotions are part of your tools; you are allowed to have them.

LI

In this day and age, we live a life, which is predominantly, associated with technology and machinery. One of the thoughts, which has become a conditioning, is that everything should come with a User Manual. Alas, we did not come with a User Manual.

It is therefore, imperative for us to acknowledge what we are, and what are the tools given to us, to live Life to the best of our ability.

Our feelings and emotions are just such tools.

In the meeting between our consciousness, mind, and physical body, there is an intersection. In the flow of our lives, there is also a flow of life within us. In other words, there is an energy that flows, or blocked, and while it flows, it has directions, volumes, and values.

Our senses provide us with input that is translated to feelings, as much as our mind does so with the spoken word and discerning.

Our emotions are Energy in Motion, for us to interpret, understand, and experience. After all, we do live an experiential existence – as said before, we are not robots.

We must firstly observe, and acknowledge them. (Next, see over leaf.)

*You are Allowed*
*Life Is A Gift*

You are allowed to
choose your
feelings & emotions.

 LII

Previously, I presented the feelings and emotions, as by-products of our sensual abilities – as an innate appearance. Yet, we may decide how to interpret them, as per our perception, for instance, someone touching you with a cold hand in the middle of winter, might be unpleasant while, the same cold hand touching your feverish forehead, winter or summer, might be a pleasant relief.

If you happen to stub your toe early in the morning, your whole day might be painted gray, and so would be any interpretation of your feelings.

On the other hand, if you happen to be an optimist, regardless of what will happen to you, you will look for the 'silver lining', and the next best step.

It has been proven in psychology that anger hardly ever pertains to one specific circumstance – that in actuality, it carries with it many parts of previous circumstances, which caused anger previously. One way to heal a current anger is to put it into perspective, to let it be measured by the immediate disturbance, and thus, reduce its volume.

The input from your senses, mind, and consciousness comes to you raw, next, with discernment, patience, and gentility, the best interpretation will appear. Take care!

 *You are Allowed  
Life Is A Gift*

You are allowed
to alter any of
your feelings &
emotions.

 LIII

In continuation, the discernment is necessary, because the gap between receiving the input, feeling the feeling, and reacting, is your sweet spot of decision making to how you are going to respond.

A funny example would be, that your beloved mother, or an esteem hostess, presented you with food that looks good, but, to your dismay, did not taste good. Would you spontaneously present her with a disgust facial expression, and insult her, or would you try to be kind, finding a gentle way to say that you do not want to eat it?

There are many examples that we can discuss, but the simple formula depends on 'long-term' versus 'short-term' behaviour. By trying to evaluate what are the ramifications of your response in the long term, you build a bridge of trust and friendship, the short-term behaviour, on the other hand, will buy you many immediate enemies.

Maturity is primarily measured by the wisdom learnt from the difference of the two behaviours.

That that your 'tools' presented you with a certain input does not mean reaction has to follow without thought – why, otherwise, do we have a mind at all?

Think of the pebble in the pond.

 *You are Allowed  
Life Is A Gift*

You are allowed to make mistakes, only they aren't mistakes, but new reference points.

 LIV

We are beings of perception; we operate by identifying things, situations, scenarios, people, and so forth. For our perception to be as accurate as possible, to benefit our responses, there are certain things that must be present.

We have to be awake, versus asleep, but also awake in the manner of acknowledging our perceptions. We have to feel good enough in order to discern that which we perceived, for example, a person with a major headache, or upset blood sugar level, or amidst explosive noises, will certainly be able to acknowledge only a fraction from what they exposed to – and therefore, should have been able to perceive.

This is how we make mistakes.

Yet, mistakes are just like a wrong step taken while dancing, and it is the illustrative dancer that might turn them to an embellishment, instead of stopping the dance altogether.

Every moment is the start point for the next; therefore, mistakes can only be used as lessons to be set as new yardsticks to measure our next step in life.

Our mind does work through associations, so a new reference point, is just that – a reference point from which to launch our next action.

 *You are Allowed Life Is A Gift*

You are allowed to
lift you eyes,
and meet with ap-
preciation
in other's eyes.

 LV

Do you remember the saying that 'The beauty is in the eye of the beholder'?

Well, as mentioned before, your value and preciousness are not!

You are a precious creation, you are part of Life, and Life would not be what it is without you, as no puzzle is complete without all its pieces. You are absolutely necessary, and all of those that belittle you, and or your value are just simply wrong – turning the mirror back to them would prove that, they too, could therefore be belittled and devalued.

If only Human Beings assume that we are all precious then, when they look at you, you will meet with appreciation in their eyes. You are of value, because you exist, and not because you have to prove, produce, beg, accomplish, or anything else before you are acknowledged.

If a man meets a grizzly bear while hiking, do you think he will doubt, even for one second, what is that bear's value, or importance? Oh No! He will give the bear the widest berth possible – and mind him without reservations. If the man is saved, he will come back, and tell his tale – carrying reverence in his voice, feeling blessed, and valued.

You, too, should be recognised for your innate value. Never doubt it.

## Epilogue

In the beginning I have said that "The Statements", here there are appearing as the chapter names, but in reality – they are statements of Truth that should be acknowledged, and understood, you will find them in Part 1 of this book.

I am quite sure that your own experience could have created many more "you Are Allowed" statements, which I would have loved to address, but then I would not leave any room for you to express yourself.

I have written some statements that it will be wonderful if you will elaborate on, you will find them in the beginning of Part 2.

The following pages I left purposefully empty for you, to enter your own statements, so you may remember the time you took for self-reflection.

You may also like to add Declarations, or any other type of statement. Feel free, and indulge in self-reflection, with the expectation that a positive outcome may always be the result of knowing thy self.

With Love & Light,

*You are Allowed*
*Life Is A Gift*

# Part 2

*You are Allowed*
*Life Is A Gift*

Joy is your inheritance.

LVI

 *You are Allowed  
Life Is A Gift*

# You are allowed to be joyful at all times.

 LVII

 *You are Allowed  
Life Is A Gift*

You were created powerful, you are entitled to your power.

 LVIII

 *You are Allowed  
Life Is A Gift*

You were created healthy, you are entitled to good health.

 LIX

*You are Allowed*
*Life Is A Gift*

# Freedom is your birthright.

LX

 *You are Allowed  
Life Is A Gift*

You are allowed
to live your life, as
you wish, without
hurting another.

 LXI

 *You are Allowed Life Is A Gift*

You are allowed to have abundance flow to you and through you.

 LXII

*You are Allowed  
Life Is A Gift*

Your giving is you
bearing fruits of
your creation.

LXIII

## You are Allowed
## Life Is A Gift

You are allowed to have life's necessities, so you can be truly nourished.

LXIV

*You are Allowed*
*Life Is A Gift*

Love is the
substance
of survival.

 LXV

 *You are Allowed*
*Life Is A Gift*

Love Thy Self, you are allowed to be loved.

 LXVI

 *You are Allowed Life Is A Gift*

Touch is the gift of existence upon Earth; you are allowed to be touched gently.

 LXVII

*You are Allowed  
Life Is A Gift*

You live in a changeable world, you are allowed to change.

LXVIII

 *You are Allowed  
Life Is A Gift*

You are allowed to grow and develop.

 LXIX

 *You are Allowed*  
*Life Is A Gift*

You are allowed to choose your own path of evolution.

LXX

 *You are Allowed*
*Life Is A Gift*

You are allowed to evolve.

 LXXI

 *You are Allowed*
*Life Is A Gift*

You are allowed
to gather your
courage.

 LXXII

*You are Allowed  
Life Is A Gift*

You are allowed to be courageous and extra-ordinary.

LXXIII

 *You are Allowed*
*Life Is A Gift*

Inspiration is
Spirit within you,
you are allowed to
have it.

 LXXIV

 *You are Allowed*
*Life Is A Gift*

You are full of light
and allowed to
shine it.

 LXXV

 *You are Allowed*
*Life Is A Gift*

You are
a beautiful creation
of The Creator, let
your beauty shine.

 LXXVI

*You are Allowed*
*Life Is A Gift*

# You are allowed to be beautiful.

LXXVII

*You are Allowed*
*Life Is A Gift*

LXXVIII

*You are Allowed*
*Life Is A Gift*

 LXXIX

 *You are Allowed Life Is A Gift*

 LXXX

 *You are Allowed Life Is A Gift*

 LXXXI

*You are Allowed*
*Life Is A Gift*

 LXXXII

*You are Allowed  
Life Is A Gift*

 LXXXIII

*You are Allowed*
*Life Is A Gift*

LXXXIV

*You are Allowed*
*Life Is A Gift*

 LXXXV

*You are Allowed*
*Life Is A Gift*

 LXXXVI

*Remember:*

*You Are Allowed,*

*Life Is A Gift*

*With Love,*

*Torry*

www.ingramcontent.com/pod-product-compliance
Lightning Source LLC
Chambersburg PA
CBHW020110020526
44112CB00033B/1126